WEATHER

Library of Congress Number: 84-26251

Library of Congress Cataloging-in-Publication Data

Kirkpatrick, Rena K.
  Weather.

  (Look at science)
  Includes index.
  Summary: Easy-to-read text and illustrations introduce facts about the weather.
  1. Weather—Juvenile literature. [1. Weather]
I. Title. II. Series.
QK981.3.K57   1985   551.5   84-26251

ISBN 0-8172-2360-6   hardcover library binding

ISBN 0-8114-6906-9   softcover binding

  4 5 6 7 8 9 10   96 95 94 93 92

WEATHER

By Rena K. Kirkpatrick
Science Consultant

Illustrated by Janetta Lewin

RSVP
RAINTREE
STECK-VAUGHN
PUBLISHERS
The Steck-Vaughn Company

Austin, Texas

What is temperature?
    You do not need coats in the summer.
In some places, you need coats in the
winter. You can feel heat during
summer and cold during winter. You
feel the difference in temperature.

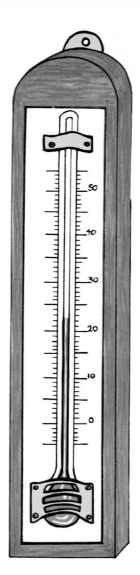

How can you measure temperature?
One way to measure temperature is with a thermometer. It measures in numbers called degrees. Use a thermometer to measure temperature in the shade. Keep a temperature chart of each day's temperature.

What might a thermometer show in winter?
The thermometer in the picture
shows that the temperature is very
cold. Ponds freeze and snow falls.
You can skate, ski, and sled.

How is ice different from water?
    Ice is frozen water. Water takes up
less space than ice. Snowflakes are
crystals of ice. Fluffy snowflakes take
up a lot of space. When a bucketful
of snow melts, only a little water is left.

What do people do when it rains?
Sometimes it rains when the sky is
dark and gray. Then people carry
umbrellas and wear raincoats.
Galoshes keep their shoes dry.

When can you see rainbows?
Sometimes the sun shines after it
rains. If you stand with your back to
the sun, you might see a rainbow.
Rainbows are made by the sun
shining through raindrops.

How can you measure the amount of
rainfall?

A funnel in a bottle can be put out in
the rain. This is called a rain gauge.
The bottle collects rainwater. You
can measure the amount of water.

cumulonimbus clouds

What do rain clouds look like?
There are many kinds of clouds.
Only some of them bring rain. Rain
clouds are dark and ragged. They are
low in the sky.

cirrus clouds

What are other clouds like?
Some clouds are high in the sky.
They are thin and wispy. You can see
blue sky through them. They are in
the sky on clear, sunny days. They
are not rain clouds.

cumulus clouds

Other clouds are puffy on top and
flat underneath. You might see them
on a nice summer afternoon. They do
not bring rain either. You might see
them after it has rained.

What is thunder and lightning?
    Lightning is like a very large electric
spark. Air moves away from the
spark. Then it rushes back and
bumps into other air. The bumping
crashes and rumbles, making
thunder.

How important is the weather?
Everybody notices weather. Sun and
clouds are part of almost every
outdoor scene that you or your
friends might paint.

What is fog?

Air is clear some days. On other days, tiny drops of water are in the air. We call the drops fog. Smoke and other tiny things in the air mix with the fog.

Sometimes fog is very thick. Ships
sound their foghorns. Airplanes
cannot take off. On the highway
warning lights flash to tell drivers to
be careful.

What is the wind like?
    Wind is another part of weather.
    Sometimes there is no wind at all.
    The air is still. It takes a long time
    for clothes to dry.

Sometimes the air moves. The wind
might blow gently. It might blow
strongly. Wind can blow from any
direction.

What is very strong wind like?
    A very strong wind is called a gale.
    Gales can break branches off trees.
    Gales can blow over garbage cans.

What is a whirlwind?

Wind that blows around in circles is called a whirlwind. Small whirlwinds blow dust and small twigs. Strong whirlwinds are called tornadoes. Tornadoes can do a lot of damage and hurt people.

21

What is a weather vane?
    Weather vanes show you the
    direction from which the wind is
    blowing. They point into the wind.

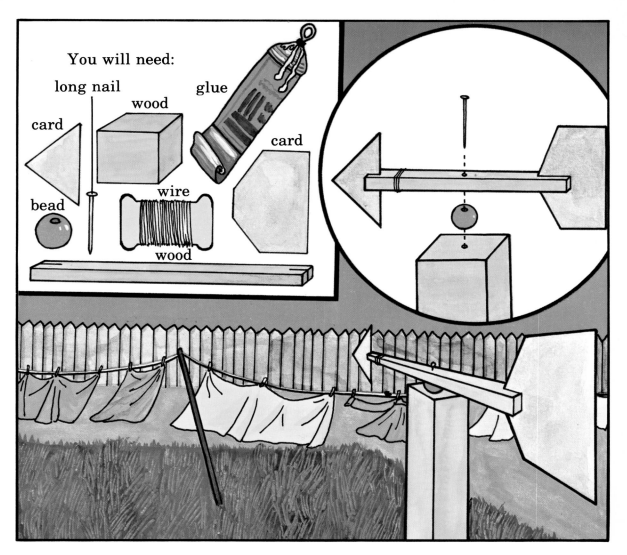

You can make a weather vane.
Follow the directions in the picture.
The pointed card will point into the
wind.

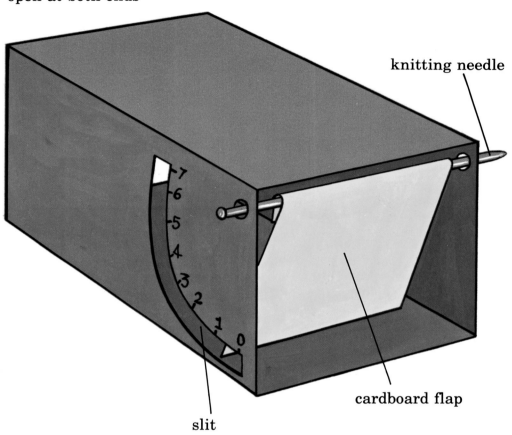

cardboard box
open at both ends

knitting needle

cardboard flap

slit

How can you measure the wind?
Build a machine like the one in the
picture. The flap should face the
wind. Numbers on the side do not
tell speed. But you can use them to
compare the wind strength from one
day to the next.

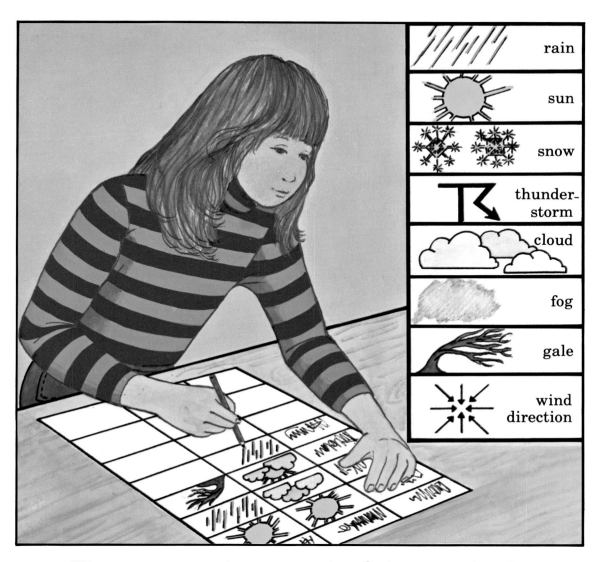

How can you keep track of the weather?
You can use symbols to keep track.
Some possible symbols are shown in
the picture. You might want to make
a daily chart.

How else can you learn about weather?
People on television tell about
weather. They have weather maps
and charts. Weather people are not
always correct.

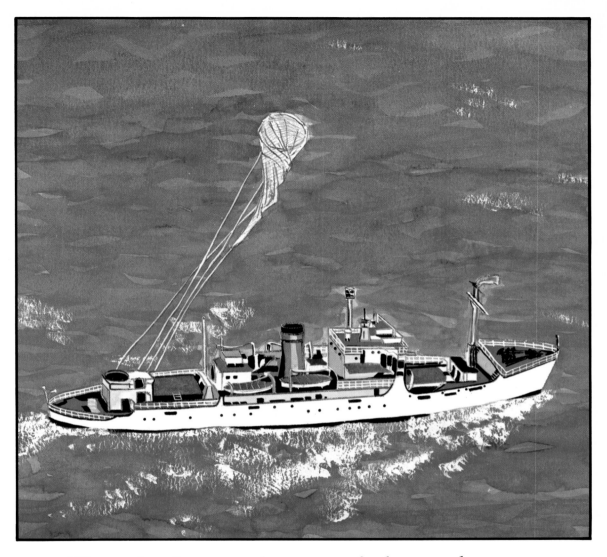

How do the weather people learn about
the weather?
    Weather ships give information about
weather. They send reports from the
ocean. The ships stay in the ocean for
a long time.

Where else do weather reports come from?
Weather satellites orbit the earth.
They send back pictures of clouds.
The pictures tell about the weather
above the land.

How is weather important to farmers?
Farmers need rain to make crops
grow. They need sun to ripen crops.
Sometimes animals get lost in the
snow.

Look at Weather Again

Temperature measures hot and cold.

Thermometers measure temperature.

Ice and snow are frozen water.

Rainbows are caused by the sun shining through raindrops.

Rain clouds are dark and low.

Lightning is like a large electric spark.

Thunder is caused by lightning.

Fog is caused by tiny water drops and other tiny things in the air.

Wind is the air that is moving.

Tornadoes are strong whirlwinds.

Weather vanes point into the wind.

Weather reporters on television use information from ships and satellites.

Farmers depend on the right weather at the right time.

Look at These
Questions About Weather

1. What are degrees on a thermometer?

2. What takes up more space—snowflakes or water?

3. Do you face toward the sun to see a rainbow?

4. What causes rainbows?

5. Are rain clouds high or low?

6. What comes first—thunder or lightning?

7. What is thunder?

8. What is fog?

9. What is wind?

10. In which direction does a weather vane point?

ANSWERS

1. The numbers that measure hot and cold.
2. Snowflakes.
3. No.
4. Sun shining through raindrops.
5. Low.
6. Lightning.
7. Air bumping together.
8. Tiny drops of water in the air.
9. Moving air.
10. Toward the wind.

Words in WEATHER

temperature
chart

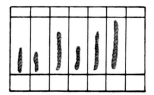

smoke

rain gauge

flash

funnel

tornadoes

wispy

weather
vane

lightning

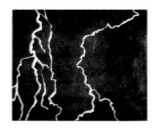

symbols

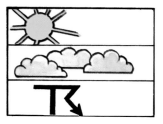